if words
could save us

Lorimer Press, Davidson, North Carolina
Book Design, Leslie Rindoks
Cover Photo, Wong Hock Weng John
Author Photo, David Crosby
Additional Acknowledgments, page 75
Printed in China

ISBN 978-0-9826171-9-9
Library of Congress Control Number: 2011933758

if words
could save us

ANTHONY S. ABBOTT

LORIMER PRESS
DAVIDSON, NC

2011

Also by Anthony S. Abbott

POETRY
The Girl in the Yellow Raincoat
A Small Thing Like A Breath
The Search For Wonder
In The Cradle of the World
The Man Who
New & Selected Poems, 1989-2009

FICTION
Leaving Maggie Hope
The Three Great Secret Things

To Susan —

— Fifty Years

TABLE OF CONTENTS

providence

ordinary time

grace

part one:
providence

The world was all before them, where to choose
Their place of rest and Providence their guide
They hand in hand with wand'ring steps and slow
Through Eden took their solitary way.

—MILTON, *Paradise Lost*

THE HAT

When I close my eyes I see the pond
and all of us skating—it must have been
December, Christmas vacation, me home

and all of us skating on the Hewitts'
pond. Ah Jenny! Do you remember?
You whizzed by, plucked my hat away

and tucked it in your red sweater.
I followed you, caught you, thrust
my hand inside the sweater, and wham!

My face stung long afterwards. I was
so young I didn't know. I was only
reaching for my hat, stupid me. Now

I wish I had known, known how to make
a game of the stealing, the reaching,
the recovery. Had I known, I might

have kissed you in the barn, deep
in the bales of hay, where we played
our innocent games of hide-and-seek.

AT THE WINDOW

He is twelve. Alone
in the lower berth

curtains closed, shade
open to the night

stars, perhaps, or the
rumble through

midwestern towns
stations deserted

some bottle perhaps
discarded

some cigarettes stomped
out. He cannot

sleep yet. He is looking
always looking

for something he
cannot name.

THIS INNOCENT SKY

On a beautiful summer morning, sky clear,
Phillipe Petit steps into the air between the towers.
On a beautiful autumn morning, sky clear,
bodies hurtle through the air between the towers.

Philippe Petit steps into the air between the towers
he tests his line as if stepping into an icy pond—
bodies hurtle through the air between the towers
strewn by the monstrous force that drove the planes.

He tests his line as if stepping into an icy pond
he walks to the center and gazes at the streets below
Strewn by the monstrous force that drove the planes
survivors cling to the narrow windows with gasping breaths.

He walks to the center and gazes at the streets below
then lies down on his line and watches passing gulls.
Survivors cling to the narrow windows with gasping breaths.
Cell phones carry burning words of love.

He lies down on his line and watches passing gulls,
police on either side attempt to call him home.
Cell phones carry burning words of love
Sirens scream from Brooklyn and beyond.

Police on either side attempt to call him home.
He smiles at them, happier than he has ever been.
Sirens scream from Brooklyn and beyond
Masses huddle on the streets their mouths agape.

He smiles at them, happier than he has ever been,
he floats beyond time, here in this innocent sky.
Masses huddle on the streets, their mouths agape
as the flames pour out, the buildings start to shake.

He floats beyond time, here in this innocent sky,
floats for thirty-seven years, his dream preserved
until the flames pour out, the buildings start to shake
the floors implode, dissolve into a cloud of noxious dust.

He floats for thirty-seven years, his dream preserved
until, on this autumn morning, sky so clear
the floors implode, dissolve into a cloud of noxious dust
where Philippe Petit, on a summer morning, once stepped into the air.

WILD OLD, MAD OLD MAN

In Memory of Howard Johnson Abbott (1904-1982)

Isn't that the point?
That he knew everything,
everything about you and me,
everything about all of us?

Because we could not bear
to keep anything from him,
because he never once judged,
never told us we were wrong.

I think he lived through us
at the end, after he'd lost
both of them, first my mother
then yours, after he nearly

drank himself to death,
then teetered dizzily on
the edge and dragged himself
back screaming to sanity

and some kind of new peace.
I think he needed us to stay
alive, needed our dark
confessions to rouse his blood.

And so that night when you
and I sat crossed legged on the
old stained rug, reading out loud
to each other his scrawled words

of help—and when we found the
other letter, the one I thought meant
he wasn't my father after all—I
cried for a long time, and you held me

and you said it wasn't true,
that it all meant something else.
I was too much like him. No one
else could have planted that seed.

FORTUNATE SON

At The Uffizi

FOR KATY SMITH ABBOTT

I stand at the Caravaggio *Bacchus*
almost touching the soft white skin
of the corrupted boy, his painted
eyebrows, his full lips. Across the room
a man and his son talk quietly
before the *Sacrifice of Isaac*,
the son the age of the screaming boy
his head pushed rudely against the rock
by his father. The knife is about
to slit his throat.
                    The son asks questions.
The father answers. I do not speak
Italian, but I understand the son's
beseeching tone. The father answers
softly, patiently, placing his arm
around the boy's shoulders. He points
to the angel, his right hand on Abraham's
wrist, holding back the knife. He points
to the old man's puzzled face and to
the ram.

The boy looks once more
at the painting. The room is silent
except for his hard breathing. "Bravo,
Angelo," he exclaims. " Bravo, Angelo,"
and reaches for his own father's hand.

THE BOY

The light falls on Matthew alone,
while the other figures remain nonchalant
—HELEN LANGDON, *Caravaggio: A Life*

In Caravaggio's *The Calling of St. Matthew*
five figures sit at a table. They have been counting
money. Two of them still are, even at the moment
Christ, in the dark, points his accusing finger
at them. St. Peter, his back to us, points also.

But, Helen Langdon, you have the light
all wrong, and as far as I can see, nobody
seems nonchalant. Yes, Matthew looks at Christ
and asks, pointing his own finger at his chest,
"Is it me?" Of course, that's right. But look
at the boy, the boy on Matthew's left,
his face bathed in the light, his innocent eyes
uplifted. He's the closest to Christ. And look
at Christ's eyes, those piercing always open
eyes, those eyes which accuse and then change
us forever, if we dare to look back.
                                        The boy
sees him. The boy's face is washed in terrible
truth, and his life will never be the same.
The two on Matthew's right keep counting.
Maybe they don't know Christ is there.
The strange one with his back to us—maybe
he's nonchalant, I don't know. He's looking

past Christ at something in the dark. But the boy
seems startled, seems to take the finger
as pointing to him as well. You too, you too
the finger says.

THE GIRL IN THE THIRD ROW

She is
      a girl on the verge
            of womanhood,

a rope bracelet
      on her left wrist
            and in her right hand

a pen making constant
      doodles, then stilled.
            Her teeth are uneven,
a chip in one.
      Her hair is a ponytail
            she tugs at. She wants

to understand
      why his words
            stir her, absurdly.

After the reading
      she will not walk
            to the front

with the others
      to ask him to sign
            her book. She will

not stand, starry-eyed,
      to hear his explanations,
            the rhythm of his voice.

Outside
      the scent of the tea olive
            follows her all the way home.

OF SANTA FINA AND THE FLOWERS THAT BLOOMED
FROM WOOD

If you didn't already know they were there
you might pass by and miss the paintings.
You might even miss the church itself.

Certainly, you'd stop to see the towers
and drink the famous San Gimignano wine
but you wouldn't have heard of Santa Fina,

a girl of ten, struck down with disease,
confined to her board, where she slept
serene and uncomplaining for five years

with rats all around her. After her parents died,
her nurse, Beldia, took care of her. Eight days
before her death St. Gregory appeared

to tell her she would die on his feast day,
and she did. In Ghirlandaio's fresco
you see the girl, fifteen, lying on her board,

all the rats but one turned into flowers,
flowers blooming from the wood itself
and then in the second painting, the miracles—

the angel, the tiny winged angel, ringing
the bells, and Beldia, the nurse, her palsied
 hand healed from Fina's touch, and the blind

choir boy holding Fina's foot to his face.
For five years she lay on the board until
 her skin became part of the board itself,

became the soil from which the flowers
sprang. The church never canonized her.
But the people did, indeed the people did.

NIGHT JOURNEY

For Nancy

"Hurry now," his sister says, get your coat
and tiptoe down the backstairs." And so
they walk out into the night,—this odd

Hansel and Gretel sitting on the train,
the conductor smiling at a girl and
boy too young for this night journey.

He trusts her, and she loves him
beyond anything, this girl brave
enough to knock on the grandparents'

door at midnight — suitcase and little
brother in hand. What does he know
about how she will pay, how she

will suffer the next day and days after
for what she has done to keep him
in the sunshine of his brown-eyed innocence.

ON THE SUBWAY

It was hot. Maybe a hundred degrees
in the stifling car. He stood, packages
in his arms, hand on the slick white
pole, bodies sweating around him.
Then it went dark, not the subway, but
he, himself. When he woke, he saw
faces looking down at him. He sat—
gathered himself. He must not
fail. He must not give in. He rose,
left the train at the next station, washed
his face in the men's room. From his
stop, he walked the six blocks home,
fearing the dark dizziness would strike
again. He could not fail. No. He walked
slowly into the house, into his room and lay
on the thin bed. He could not sleep, not yet,
There was dinner, and the small talk
of families over peas and potatoes. Then,
mercifully, bed. For fourteen hours, he slept.
In the morning when he woke, the dark
was gone. It was never mentioned. He
would hold it in his heart and wait
for another day. He would take ten
breaths and be strong. He would not fail.
Not today, not tomorrow, not ever.

"BEATA POPOLANA"

Catherine of Siena, 1347-1380,
"the blessed one of the people"

She eludes me, eludes us all really
this girl who called the Pope himself "dolcissimo
Babbo mio" — and the thing was he listened
to her. They all listened to her—

Popes, cardinals, bishops, priests, soldiers—
criminals before death, cursing God
with their last breaths until she changes them—
She kneels by Niccolo di Toldo

takes his severed head in her hands and sees
him enter Paradise, this simple girl—
Catherine Benincasa, the daughter
of a wool dyer. When she was six

God spoke to her, and she became the bride
of Christ for life, this simple dyer's daughter,
the twenty-third and youngest child of parents
who never understood—how could they?

She held lepers in her arms, she kissed
cancerous breasts of women who hated her,
thought she was proud. The doctors of the church
came to her small cell to lay traps for her.

During her ecstasies they poked her
with knives and scissors to see if she was
faking it. She never budged. Later
when she woke she felt the pain.

They went away amazed. She had no arrogance,
no fear, no anger. Only love and an ear
for Christ's voice. For years she ate nothing
but consecrated bread. "Father, I'm hungry,"

she cried to her confessor. "For the love
of God, give my soul its food." Her followers
increased. "Mamma," they called her,
and carried her to Avignon and back

to bring her "Babbo" home to Rome. Here she died,
her face radiant as an angel's, this girl,
this slight young girl who feared nothing.
God loves everyone, she said. Everyone.

THE BLESSING

"I will not let you go unless you bless me"

GENESIS 32:26

After the torn sinews
and the joint

displaced, the hollow
of the thigh

made sacred, what did
he want

but some final blessing
at the end

a thousand white petals
falling

hand over hand over
hand

the rain, the rain
the rain.

IN GRAND CENTRAL STATION

The boy looks up at the stars in the Upper Concourse.
Usually he is entranced by the way they make
the shapes of creatures and mythic heroes—
hunters and bears and flying horses. But today

he has no heart for them. He has waited on the bench
by Gate 32 for half an hour. He has watched
for his mother's blue coat with the torn hem
and the white scarf she wears on rainy days.

He is starting to cry and he does not like
to cry at all. It scares him here among
these strangers. He has called her hotel.
The woman at the desk said she was out.

Perhaps she is on her way, caught in a mad
swirl of late afternoon traffic, a crush
of trucks and multi-colored cabs, yellow
and green and checkered. Perhaps she

is on the subway, trapped by a red light
between stations. He wipes his eyes
with his handkerchief, and then he feels
for the first time the icy touch of death.

She will not come at all. She will never
come, and he might sit on this wooden
bench until he grows old, and still
she will not come. She will never know

how he has counted on this small good
time between then, this time that will
never be. He stands, puts his tears away
in the pocket with his used handkerchief.

At the glass booth he will request a schedule.
He will go back to school, he will collect
his A's and spread them on the smooth
palm of his heart. He will live.

NECESSARY MUSIC

After I left
the flowers on my mother's grave—
calla lilies, freesia,
the enormous, fragile
peony—I asked my
heart for her forgotten
voice. Was it soft,
like the lilt
of her Georgia
childhood? Or more
like the dirt red notes
of her piano, out of key
from the smoke of too
many bars?

I search for the music
of her voice
in the rustle
of the naked limbs.

The wind says wait.

COMING OF AGE

On the morning of my twenty-first birthday
my sister left for California.
Suitcases, boxes, tied to the roof,
she waved goodbye and vanished.

My sister left for California
taking with her the only home I'd known.
She waved goodbye and vanished.
In the back seat the children read comics.

She took away the only home I'd known.
In my city, snow graying on the dirty streets.
In the back seat the children read comics,
in their old apartment dust and the flicker of grease.

In my city, snow graying on the dirty streets—
nowhere to go now, nothing to be done.
In their old apartment dust and the flicker of grease.
Where do you live, my friends at college ask?

Nowhere to sleep now, nothing to be done
except take the train back to school.
Where do you live, my friends at college ask?
In the regions of the mind, in my shuttered heart.

I take the train back to school,
closing my old coat around my neck.
In the regions of my mind, in my shuttered heart
I watch for the star that played at Bethlehem.

I close my old coat around my neck
and walk the sixty stairs to my tower room.
I watch for the star that played at Bethlehem
and kneel in silence by my narrow bed.

Nothing comes but the spinning of wheels.
She waved goodbye and vanished
tossed her cigarette out the window
on the morning of my twenty-first birthday.

WINTER PANTOUM

on the night of the third snow
I walk out alone
upward through the bare branches
the white makes a long path

I walk out alone
the falling flakes on my face
the white makes a long path
for my nearly silent footsteps

the falling flakes on my face
the dark is welcome and expected
my nearly silent footsteps
following the lost trail of you

the dark is welcome and expected
the leaves of the magnolia like white blossoms
I follow your lost footsteps
I gaze at the lighted windows of homes

the leaves of the magnolia like white blossoms
the morning sun dazzles the eyes
I gaze at the dark windows of homes
wind blows snow from slanted roofs

the morning sun dazzles the eyes
I walk once more on the frozen street
wind blows snow from slanted roofs
patience is the last harbor of the heart

I walk once more on the frozen street
I search through the bare branches
patience is the last harbor of the heart
on the morning after the third snow

part two:
ordinary time

*Tell me, what is it you plan to do
with your one wild and precious life?*

—Mary Oliver, "The Summer Day"

AT THE LAKE, SUMMER EVENING

A full moon
      luminous, large,
            rises

over the eastern trees.
      In the west, thunder-heads.
          The sky darkens.

I turn the boat
      toward home,
          lightning behind me.

On the lift
      the boat sits steady.
          I snap the cover into place.

She is dry now,
      snug against the weather.
          The rain begins to fall.

Another crash of thunder.
      I raise my head to the angry sky.
          The moon is gone.

In my house the lights flicker.

THE GIRL WITH A PEARL EARRING

The mouth
is the first thing
the way

the lips open
the lower so lovely
sensuous

the tongue just
showing
between as if

she would speak
her thoughts no
her feelings

that is really what
the painting says
Jesus look at

the eyes which
tell us all tell us
of something private

she cannot speak
or will not
but the artist

knows God those
eyes looking
as the critics say

into our
space and the
lovely high cheek

bones and all
the hair
hidden under the blue

turban and the exquisite
extra drip of paint
on the earring

HOUSE OF CARDS

from The Parable of the Great Feast, LUKE 14

Once there was a man who gave
a party. He invited the top of the deck.
The Kings and Queens,
Jacks and tens, and, of course,
the Aces, those powers behind
even the Kings themselves, though
we all know it's the Queens who run
the show. The point is none of them
came. That's right, none of them

The Kings were busy in the walled
 city, in the compound, deconstructing
 their missiles, and the Queens,
 the Queens were always moaning
about how overcommitted they were.
The Queens were sad, but busy or sad, it was
still a no, and the Jacks, the Jacks were cooking
up stuff, making plans, hatching the eggs
of desire and circumlocution. They were,
you might say, moving.

And the tens were so insecure, they just
sat there polishing their little hearts or
spades. They wanted to look good for
the Queens. They wanted to move up,
get a face, one of those cool one-eyed
Jack poses. So who was this guy anyway?
A nine at best.
But the guy, as I understand the story, was—

well, I know this comes as some surprise—
God. He just looked like a nine. And he was
really mad, and he told his servants, the eights,
to go out in the town, where all the new
subdivisions were, and find some sevens
and sixes, and then go down to Affordable Housing
and the bus station and the Wal-Mart
for some threes and fours, and most of all,
God said, invite the twos. By God, God laughed,
those twos are the best. And don't forget the fives.
The fives might need a little extra persuading,
those skeptical fives.

              And there it was, all those
beautiful low numbers crowding around the pool out back
drinking beer and eating chips and salsa, some of the threes
and sixes mixing it up, the sevens and fours
playing drums and guitars, the fives singing chorus.
And the twos, God bless the twos, they were
if you haven't guessed it, the lovers. The twos
always came in sets. God liked the hearts
and diamonds best, but he loved them all.
And then, at the witching hour, or whatever
hour you like, God told some stories, and started
crying and wiping his eyes because he was so
happy to have them all there.

And as for the royalty, and as for the royalty,
and those slick behind the scenes Aces, well
there would be some wailing and gnashing
of teeth, just like the Good Book says. That's
what I heard from those who were there.
Two twos told me so.

THE YOUNG

look right through
you

as if you are
not

there. Maybe some
swishing

of the tail could compel
attention

or better still a quick
thrust

of the forked
tongue

as if to say,
"Dudes,

I'm, hey, you know,
like

a real, fucking
person."

MISS CLARITY COMES TO THE PARTY

in her high-necked dress,
stockings and sensible shoes.
Hair curled under, tight
against her neck. Pearls, good
old-fashioned pearls. She's
a smart one, through and through.
Indeed she is. She has radar
for everything. She watches
eyes and the small touch of
even fingers as a glass is passed
from hand to hand. She knows.
The young blond man, lounging
in the corner, back against the wall,
chatting so amiably with the dark
woman in the print skirt and the
bare feet, on this warm summer
evening. Circumspection is her
motto. Latin. circum—around—
specare—to look. Of course, that's
it. I mean, if you're looking around,
no one's got anything on you, do they,
Miss Clarity? Did you catch that?
I changed persons from third to second.
to first. Now there's a peccadilo, from
the Latin—peccare—to sin. You got me.

WASHINGTON: IN THE DARK PLACES

In this year of global warming
when Al Gore sent out his warning
all the polar bears were swimming
'cause their ice caps were all thinning

In April it snowed all across America.
In the Midwest, across the Great Lakes
to Vermont and Maine, up the Appalachian
corridor. It snowed, and in the deep South
the peaches froze, the strawberries froze,
and in Florida even the oranges froze.
The coldest April on record.

In the deep recesses, the dark basement
of the White House, the President
chuckled with glee. He was right.
There was no global warming.
It was the coldest April on record.

He pursued the war with new vigor.
He vetoed bills, and swore never
to back down. It was the coldest
April on record.

IN YOUR IMAGE

The weariness of numbers
     and the sickening smile
          of the politician

on the face of Newsweek magazine,
     orange, yellow stickum
          on the heads of wild birds.

Ah, Christ. I want the touch
     of your hand on my arm
          I want my finger in your wounds

Thomas that I am. I kneel
     at the altar. You stand
          before me, cup in hand.

Do you hear the clang of bells
     on Wall Street, voices
          burning, anger

like grill-blackened meat.
     You stand, cup in hand
          you bend to me

this is my blood, you say.
     I reach out
          and touch

the withdrawing air.

AT THE CHRISTMAS CELEBRATION

of the book club that doesn't read
books, the ladies introduce their men
who with the ladies consume much
wine and enjoy staccato bursts
of conversation. The poet is baffled.

He cannot make words in this festive
scene. He moves from room to room
spinning in his mind like a dervish.
Living room, dining room, kitchen,
den, guest bedroom, and back again.

He listens to the break-neck talk,
the roars of laughter at what must
be something he has completely
missed once more. He can make words
from the burning leaves of the soul

but this he cannot fathom. What
can they think of to say that brings
such smirks, such grins, such open
mouthed chewing? What news
from Bethlehem? Where do the kings

lodge tonight? Will they tell all
to Herod? Who will there be to warn
the children, to cry to the nursing
mothers—pluck up your babes
and leave before the soldiers rattle

in with their copper armor and their
thick heads. The poet wants to shout
"Fire!" and watch them all disperse
into the tumbling rain and fog out there.
But he keeps his peace. Instead he

knocks on God's door three times
to give thanks for the strange child
who must have hammered nails himself
before the nails hammered him
and sent the world reeling into darkness.

IF NICE IS ENOUGH

cut out the words of
endearment

snip, snip, sweetheart
snip, darling

then the lovely interlocked
letters of lovers

beads on a rosary
and the smells

of the fecund September
earth

its sturdy, sweet
steadfastness

and the moans to the blue
moon

in the December
snow

the gray wolf of
anger

the black stallion of
passion

the howls of the lost
old man

Lear and Cordelia
the heath

cut these out and
what remains

is quite respectable
one might

even say quite
nice

MONDAY AFTER EASTER

The gray stain of rain
pouring down.

I stand at your grave.
For a long time

nothing but the ragged
gasps

of my own breath.
I want.

But angels don't have
wings

do they, my darling?
Only mud-colored

shoes and scars from centuries
of open eyes.

We've seen too much
you and I.

All right, then. So be it.
The red bow

on the wreath stains
the stone below.

NOLI ME TANGERE

"Do not touch," says the guard. I step back,
startled. I did not know I was so close.
Perhaps her name is Mary, this woman,
Vermeer's woman in blue reading a letter.
How she loves him, how her eyes take the words
into her heart, how fixed she is. How
I love her. "Do not touch," says the guard again.
And then in my mind that other Mary
her eyes fixed on the cave mouth, the open
tomb, her eyes wet with tears. Where is my Lord,
she asks. Where have you taken him. And she
sees the form of her beloved, her Jesus,
walking toward her. She rushes, arms out
to take him to her heart. "Do not touch," he says.
And she comes on, comes on, to hold him now
and forever. "Do not touch," he says again
and the guard says, "Do not touch." My eyes blur.
The face of the woman before me, Mary's face,
my fingers reaching, reaching after empty air.

IN THE QUIET SPACES

At the dinner table
        talk spills in rivulets
drips like melted wax on candlesticks
        the man sits suspended.

The curtains whisper in the dark room
        where the wash of waves
pushes against his memory.

Much laughter. A man
        smiles, gestures grandly
and a woman nods, gaudy necklace
        leaps in agreement.

The man bends to pick
        a brown glove
from the dark path. The dog waits patiently.

Yes, a bald man echoes,
        we met on the internet
we both loved travel

If Jesus came today
        where would he set his feet?
If I saw him, would I know?

It is best to exchange your money in advance
        do the pills for jet lag work?
No, ties are not necessary.

Outside a million stars are burning
*   I am dying, Egypt, dying*
promises to keep, and miles to go. . .

The wine is best drunk cold
        sweaters are advised in the evening
A waiter smiles in dull agreement.

ELEPHANTS WALKING

Tonight in Pilanesburg National Park
the elephants own the roads.
We learn patience as their guests.
They walk the roads in front of us.

The elephants own the roads.
Their trunks lolling back and forth
They walk the roads in front of us
ears flapping, tails swishing the flies.

Their trunks lolling back and forth
they take their own sweet time
ears flapping, tails swishing the flies
nowhere to go, no clocks, no digitals.

They take their own sweet time.
Dum-de-dum, down the road they march
Nowhere to go, no clocks, no digitals.
their huge rear legs like ancient columns.

Dum-de-dum, down the road they march
snatching the nicest branches from the trees,
their huge rear legs like ancient columns
reminding us the road is theirs, not ours.

Snatching the nicest branches from the trees
these gentle giants still our stupid greed
reminding us the road is theirs not ours.
The tar feels warm against their tired feet.

These gentle giants still our stupid greed
we learn patience as their guests.
The tar feels warm against their tired feet
tonight in Pilanesburg National Park.

RECITING THE EMPTY POEMS

The man who drives
        alone in his car
                recites his poems

to the adagio of Mozart
        fitting the words
                to each note

each ivory key
        a beat, he recites
                his poems to Dvorak

to Tchaikovsky,
        to the thrust
                of the full orchestra

he charges down
        the road alone
                his free left foot

beating time,
        his right hand
                conducting

lost in a maze
        of snaky memories
                wished now, wanted now

driving down the road
    alone, reciting
        the empty poems.

YOU, RAIN

thrum your fingers
on my roof. I rejoice
in your rhythm.

The small plants,
tired, bent over,
rejoice, and the trees
rejoice and the purple
flowers outside my window.

We have waited
and waited through
the dry nights, the words
lost in the swirling dust,
throat swollen in yellow
silence.

Today, I stood on the
side of the road and laughed.
Oh yes, and I stood on the
side of the road and wept

and threw my head back
and took you in my mouth
into my eyes, on the lobes
of my ears, took you on
my tongue and tasted you.

And gave thanks for your
touch, and now I lie in my
still room listening to
your fingers thrumming
on my roof, healing,
healing the jagged wound
of time.

part three:

grace

Most tears are grace. The smell of rain is grace.
Loving somebody is grace. Have you ever tried to
love somebody?

—Frederick Buechner

BEFORE

there was only
decency and the murmur
of small streams

now the whole earth
is green with spring
grass and the rush

of great waters.

THE GIFTS OF THE HEART ARE HOLY

In September my neighbor's
  dock glows gold
    at sunset.

Already the sound
  of acorns on the roof breaks
    the silence of the night.

The scientist says
  we don't need God
    that the universe

explains itself.
  I look at the lake
    and the darkening sky.

I have no words for this.
  If not God, then
    only that

"indifferent and dividing blue"
  as the poet says.
    The gifts of the heart

are holy.
  Wash the nightsweat
    from your palms.

Begin.
  There is always
    someone listening.

GOING HOME:

A POEM IN MEMORY OF THOSE NORTH CAROLINA WRITERS
WHO HAVE GONE BEFORE US

—Weymouth Center, July, 2009

Late afternoon. I lie in the long grass and wait
for words. The still white clouds mock me. Then,
unexpectedly, the sound of music. I sit up. From
an open window upstairs, the clear sounds
of Dvorak. I know these notes like I
know the timbers of my own soul. Yes.

The English horn sings the theme, and sings it
yet again, with the bass clarinet. And then
the strings enter, like a prayer. Take me home,
Lord, take me home. Now the clarinets,
and the horns like faith answer. Then the strings
whisper softly, yes, and again, yes.

I see Graham Jackson, tears running down his black
cheeks, Graham Jackson, in full dress uniform, playing
"Goin' Home" for his beloved Franklin Roosevelt, and then
the farmers, young and old, black and white, all
of them poor, who loved the only man they had
ever known as President of the United States, hundreds
standing on the hills of Georgia and the Carolinas
watching the train go by with the body of their lost
leader, watching the train take him home. "Goin' home"
say the English horns again, and then the clarinet returns.

Here I am, listening, images surfacing—the trim brick walks
of my beloved town, the green hills to the west, rising
and falling like the strings, the waves on the outer
banks crashing like the cymbals, then sliding back
like the clarinets. I see the faces of my friends, I hear
the voices of the poets who have gone before, their words
rising again. Dark skinned and light, old and young, male
and female, children of the valleys and the mountains,
children of the coast and the Piedmont. I am here, they say,
I have made the path for you, and I am still here, my words
as true as the rock face of Cold Mountain.

The music soars and for a moment there is light. The whole
orchestra together in hope. Then the English horn alone,
mournful, and the strings so soft, almost a whisper.
The strings carry our love over the hills to the sea,
 the horns offer it to the sky, and the strings set it aloft.
 It is done. They have gone home, and who and what
they are we carry within ourselves. The evening comes.
I rise from the grass and walk toward the open window.

EARLY SPRING

That moment when
      the light green
            just brushes

the edges of the canvas
      and the yellow
          of forsythia
steals the eye
      from the blue sky
         and it is too soon

for the torn cross
      of dogwoods
         and the tight

buds of azaleas
      still wait in their
         small cocoons.

Last night
      when the moon came out
         after the rain

I thought of you.

KNIFE BLADE OF THE NEW MOON

1.

He wakes one day astonished
        to the burgeoning spring.
                The white azaleas

doomed it seemed
        from the deadening drought
                now whiter than ever before

in full profusion
        on the front lawn
                Even the light green

of the coming leaves
        just created, just born
                their small fingers

reaching out to the blue air
        the frogs in the pools
                the cardinals chasing

each other through the holly
        drunk on berries
                and the girls on the campus

their legs white
        from their long winter rest
                spreading their quilts

on the front lawn
    and reading Plato
        their eyes closed

their long hair dangling
    over the Allegory of the Cave.

2.

For a long time he had forgotten
    such things. He had walked
        with his head down, eyes askance.

Now he stands in the rain,
    mouth open
        tasting the wetness.

He kneels on the willing earth
    places his face
        in the long spring grass

and smells earthsmell,
    greensmell, Godsmell.
        He looks up.

He remembers. The knife blade
    of the new moon cuts
        through the parting clouds.

THE BELOVED SON

He had still one other, a beloved son; finally he sent him to them, saying,
"They will respect my son." ...and they took him and killed him and cast
him out of the vineyard. What will the owner of the vineyard do? He will
come and destroy the tenants, and give the vineyard to others.

—MARK 12: 6, 8-10

I think now about the father, the owner
of the vineyard, there in the other country
looking out over the wall of his compound
and seeing the procession, the small
procession of beasts, one bearing the remains
of his son. At first he is not sure. Then
he sees the coat, the mantle he had given
him for his coming of age—the blue one,
the mantle covering the torn body slung
sideways over the horse's back.

For days he mourns, he cries his rage
to the skies, he wails and shreds
his garments. Oh, they will pay. They
will pay for this. His revenge will be
terrible. He will gather his troops
and he will destroy them all, utterly.

How much he had loved this boy,
this easy boy with his high smile,
this boy who said, "Yes, Father, I
will go, and they will listen to me."

He measured his hatred in hours.
He would quarter them, pour
boiling oil on their innards
and throw them screaming over
their own walls, as they had thrown
his son. His vengeance would be sweet.

But then the angel came, or something
like the angel, something in the night
in dreams..."forgive...they know not
what they're doing..."

What will the owner of the vineyard do?

I see him kneeling at the dark gate
in the mud, soft after the spring rains.
"Pray with me," he calls to the tenants.
"This is the body of my son, broken
for you.." And he reaches high, holding
in his hands the blue mantle, and the tenants
come forth, weeping, and the father takes
each of them in his arms and kisses them.

And the vineyard, they say, brought forth
much fruit.

VERMEER: WOMAN IN BLUE READING A LETTER

It is all
in the letter
she reads

with such quiet
passion not
anger not fear

not even joy
but utter
concentration

such absolute focus
on the words
his words.

How she grasps
the edges
of the paper

so tenderly with
both hands
one is not enough

for this giving of her
whole self
to a moment

for which she has
waited quietly
patiently, forever.

THE MAN WHO DIDN'T BELIEVE IN LUCK

No such thing as luck. It was all hard work,
toughness, the early bird. He laughed. Let softies
believe in luck. He'd just get up earlier
and beat the slackers to work.

                              Then his daughter
died, in the blackness of the night. He awoke
on Easter Monday without her. The dark
stretched before, the long thin legs of time marched
slowly onward. He snarled at luck. He snarled
at chance. I'll show them, he growled. Show them what?

He danced dizzily into the dust of despair.
He slammed the door on his bloody toes
and looked for signs. In Vietnam the body
bags multiplied. The heart is a stone.

He wandered in the desert of dark dreams,
digging in the hard earth. What was down there
anyway? The hard black nugget of fame?
Stupid, he thought, and again, stupid.

When the first touch came, the tears came with it.
He had kept them all in his back pocket with the memories
of childhood. He began to talk, small words
like the first hint of dawn before sunrise.

The muse stretches the legs of time. She opens
her mouth and yawns and stretches again, and starts

to move. She knows everything. Wounded words
limp forward into the river of grace.
He knows this now. We bend the knee of the heart
to the risen Christ, who loves us. She is
somewhere with him. We deserve nothing. We
earn nothing, but we are loved just the same.
Nothing to be done except to give it back.
Yesterday's tears are tomorrow's promises.

GRIEF

1.
For years he stood stiff as a brass candlestick
while the leaves danced down the street
in their coats of many colors, and the branches

bent before the wind. At the ocean once
he lay awake all night just to hear the waves
crash against the splintered beach, the dark

erasure of time falling back through sand.
In a picture on his shelf, his young daughter
balances her perfect body on her

haunches, her feet flat on the level sand
as she spells her name in shells before
the surging tide erases her.

2.
Alone in his car he listens to Mozart
and grieves for the lovely friend he drove
to doctors every week, gone now into

the white ash of forgetfulness. He wails
aloud to the flute and the swirling violins,
wails for the western star, sinking in the

cloud-edged sea, for the child he once was
reaching through the bars of his candied
crib, fingers spread outward, listening

to the rain on the roof, the thunder,
the parents down the hall asleep
under the dark crosses of their covers.

MODERN ART

Sliced oranges, pink
sea shells

a woman's face, crescent
moon with stars

black on black on
black.

A touch on my
shoulder.

It's all right, you say,
move on.

UNHOLY WHISPERS

because I
did not

*an aged man
is but a*

could not
do not

*paltry thing
unless*

will not
still I

*soul clap its
hands*

need I
want

*and sing
and louder sing*

the grass
says yes

*for every tatter in its
mortal dress*

these unholy
whispers

IF WORDS COULD SAVE US

if words could save us (and they can, my darling)
i would whisper in the chambers of your ears
every wistful sound (like the warblings
of the wood thrush) until (my wren) even
the small boys whose voices are like angels
would cry for more, and you (my swan) would sigh
like the sun setting behind the ocean floor.

if touch could save us (and it does, my dove)
i would take the wounds of time and touch them all
until the soul (my sweetness) shines with the light
of God in the newness of now. Healing is
the only language of love (my lamb) for
wherever we have touched, the tree that grows
will be blessed (my bliss) and the fruit of that tree
will be life (my love) the fruit of that tree will be life.

Acknowledgements

Thank you to the journals and anthologies where some of these poems first appeared, sometimes in slightly different form:

Pembroke: "The Hat," "Night Journey," "If Nice is Enough," "Beata Popolana"

Anglican Theological Review: "Fortunate Son," "Noli Me Tangere"

Kakalak: "Of Santa Fina and the Flowers that Bloomed From Wood," "In Grand Central Station"

Christianity and Literature: "The Boy"

Tar River Poetry: "The Girl with a Pearl Earring"

Cold Mountain Review: "House of Cards"

Main Street Rag: "The Young"

Pine Straw: "At the Christmas Celebration"

Journey Without: Charlotte Writers Club Anthology, Volume 4: "Washington: In the Dark Places"

Iodine: "Knife Blade of the New Moon," "Vermeer: Woman in Blue Reading a Letter"

LUCK: A Collection of Facts, Fiction, Incantations & Verse: "The Man Who Didn't Believe in Luck"

Author's Note

The production of this book has been a special joy for me, not only because of the poems themselves which I always consider a gift of the spirit, but because people have always asked me to record my poems, and now I have done it. I would like to thank Evan Richey of Ovation Sound in Winston-Salem, North Carolina for creating the CD and helping me with his fine-tuned ear in each step of the process. I would like to thank Ann Campanella for reading the manuscript and Beth Swann for her astute criticism of particular poems. Most of all I would like to thank Leslie Rindoks for her stunningly beautiful cover and design; and Allison Elrod for her thoughtful work as editor and publicist, as well as her wisdom and steadfast support throughout this project.

Anthony S. Abbott

Anthony S. Abbott is the Charles A. Dana Professor Emeritus of English at Davidson College where he served as Department Chair from 1989 to 1996. He is the author of four critical studies, two novels and six books of poetry, including the Pulitzer nominated *The Girl in the Yellow Raincoat*. His awards include the Novello Literary Award for *Leaving Maggie Hope* (2003), and the Oscar Arnold Young Award for *The Man Who* (2005) as well as the Irene Blair Honeycutt Award for Lifetime Achievement in the Arts. He lives in Davidson, North Carolina with his wife, Susan.